THIS IS NOT A
FRANK OCEAN
COVER ALBUM

THIS IS NOT A FRANK OCEAN COVER ALBUM

ALAN CHAZARO

Black
Lawrence
Press

www.blacklawrence.com

Executive Editor: Diane Goettel
Chapbook Editor: Kit Frick
Book and Cover Design: Amy Freels
Cover Art: "Sinking" by Iselle Kim. Used with permission.

Published 2019 by Black Lawrence Press.
Printed in the United States.

For the brothers who raised me,
who I was raised with,
and who I've helped in raising;
this is for you.

Contents

580 West

Listen: this is scorpions in the dark, the buzz of moonlight
catching almost-white teeth. This is hyphy as we glide

the Bay Bridge, bone and cartilage scribbling fences with tattered
alphabets. This is the curve of question marks, a nearby fog

mixing my breath. I am revolving around a certain body right now.
There's a black Acura breaking the boulevard, bending sound

corners. Briana says she wants to catch a vibe. Jerome
says you can catch these hands. I float around the city while Odd

Future grooves into an empty background. Lately, my outside is more
inside. Lately, blunt smoke waxes my tongue. A group of teenagers

are practicing free throws in the dark while adults get drunk
and throw money at the corner bar. What are they preparing

for? Lake Merritt looks upside down from this angle. Have you ever
wondered how palms trees fortress themselves in a city of asphalt

and dead starlight? Golden State is scripted onto the chest of my jersey's fabric.
Tonight my head is in another space. I am somewhere between Gap

corduroys and a black hoodie. I am above the surface but feeling
undertaken. Breath is an orchestra of unbroken body parts. Breakages

depend on how fragile you've become. I heard about a white woman
who called the police because her neighbor was breaking

into himself. Translation: he was entering
his apartment building. Fill in the blanks. Lately there are too many

blanks to be filled. Yesterday I asked where it all went. I woke up
to the rose dust of another planet in my backyard. I run the hills around

my apartment and look at a faraway skyline. It feels like it doesn't belong
to anyone except those who don't deserve it. I remember being sixteen

riding in Andrei's Cadillac, smashing freestyles
while we cruised freeways, steering into unknowns. I don't stay

connected much, rarely charge my phone, especially when driving
at night, but here we find ourselves. I shouldn't text in a foreign language

when I can barely hold my own fingers. These flowers are too loud for me;
I can hear them singing off-key with my windows rolled all the way up.

A Millennial Walks into a Bar and Says:

Let's start off with a Disney movie because why
shouldn't we? The one where the boy gets sucked
into the game his father created. Virtual

reality. And let's consider how there is an invisibility
to everything. How voices can break air-
waves across oceans slapping coastlines. And let's disregard

tsunami ripples. Who takes responsibility for this, anyway?
It's an American thing to scream out *take no prisoners* in public. If not,
it should be. Think of national security threats. Unidentified hackers

who break codes. I asked my students what they thought
about this and they told me about plaid shirts, the lag
of internet, *Wreck-It Ralph*. Excuse me, I've mentioned

another Disney movie I haven't seen. Honestly,
I worry about oil pipelines in North Dakota.
About congress evil-scheming behind

our noses. They are planting lemon trees
in our backyard like it's okay but this is approval
by majority so sit back and watch that shit grow. I apologize

if nothing bothers you; I am easily bothered. This brings me back
to lemon trees and oil pipelines. Doesn't it seem
like *Planet of the Apes*? What if Charlton Heston was telling us

something important when he said *I'm sending my last signal
to Earth before we reach our destination*?
That's a rough paraphrase. What isn't rough?

When they discovered neon it was accidental.
When they discovered continents it was accidental.
When they discovered us it was accidental.

Maybe not. Maybe I'm saying history
isn't orchestrated by a perfect god.
We are by-products of earthquakes. And English

is commonly spoken everywhere. Does anyone care
it started with rape? Often,
I speak in another voice. Maybe

it's yours. I apologize. I apologize
for apologizing so much. In the 1940s
a group of teenage boys were treated

as experiments by the SS. I learned about them
while touring a death camp in Oranienburg.
How the Germans kept them for *scientific purposes*.

How those boys outlived the German lieutenants. Poetic
justice, some might say. Meanwhile in the South Bronx, teenagers
built cultures from wax while DJing inside broken

down project buildings and spitting fluids into crowds
who kept their hands up until the break of dawn. A breaking
dance motion. Contortions of the spirit. Head spins. Nothing

like US military drones missing their targets. Nothing.
But everything like jazz quartets. In New Orleans
there are streets that have retained the noises of ghosts:

Tchoupitoulas; Calliope; St. Claude. Find me
there. I want to remix the wrongs and make a mixtape
of imperfection. I want to put this in your stereo

and let your older brother get drunk to it, let your grandmother
fall asleep to it. Dreams are the origin of an end. Think
about flying cars and robots in movies that act and move

fakingly real. Am I wrong? I really can't say
I'm Mexican just as I really can't say
I'm American. Someone built this bridge between me. They carved

hyphens from the air for me to cross. Not just the crossing
you might be thinking of. But the sort that can birth multiples:
national borders, puzzles, holy crucifixions, movements

across disparate bodies. I apologize again. I just did that thing
when you use a word in your definition to define another word. I'm sure
language is empired from mistakes so I'd rather

not take this to you. It might stifle what my friend Stan
calls *moon-guzzling*. Instead, keep jogging until you reach the edge
of yourself. And jump off. And find pleasure between your falling

breaths. The week before Obama's presidency ended we drove
to Half Moon Bay. 80s synthpop and a flood
of lo-fi on the stereo. I found a decayed bunker on a cliffside

with aqua graffiti letters that spelled *INNA TRIBE*. Yesterday,
I ate ribs at a mom and pop's in South Hayward. The talk of teaching,
of weddings, the slow goodness of slow-cooked BBQ inside us. Nobody

flinches. Imagine Tongo and MK Chavez hurling poems
at the heads of protestors in our streets while something burns
in the near distance; strange horizons to remind us of unbroken nights;

a reminder to drive slow and pump your brakes; visions of Kanye;
Shakir from the Lower Bottoms singing Italian operas at California
house parties. Not like what you see on television. Or maybe

it is. We were born here and raised up like the Redwoods. Who asked?
Moving on, our neighbors are new and the old ones just moved out.
Not always by choice. How does a space change over time? It's just time

they say. I don't talk with Ma much because she bounces around,
this time to LA. Video games are her pleasure. In *Dragon Age Inquisition*
she plays as a character who hunts dragons and has sex with other players—

she explained this to me, though I've never owned a PS4. In *WIRED* magazine
you can read about two sisters from Seattle, ages 9 and 11, who built a Do-It-Yourself
spacecraft from simple materials and used a GoPro to capture its ascent

into the blindness of space. It's all on YouTube. I wonder
if our imaginations become wrinkled and weary with age. I wonder
if things are really things. I bet all things eventually change

when resisted (i.e. Civil Rights). How this can all pour
from my fingers in a matter of minutes like outdated
newspapers. We mostly use Facebook as a source of news anyways.

Entertainment doesn't hide itself from us very well. At the gym,
why do we look so discomfortable? At bars, why
do we look so discomfortable? This is rude of me to ask on a first date,

I've been told. Perhaps the salad would have been a better choice.
Locally foraged, says the 8-pt. font menu. Some of us would rather eat strawberries
at home while watching Trevor Noah. Note to self: do this on a Wednesday night.

Self-Portrait as American

I say *fuck*
because it feels right
about now,
and I say *love* because
what wrong
could it bring?
I haven't shot a pistol
since my stepdad
flung his Desert Eagle
from the bedroom and took us
to burst freedom as kids.
The smell of sulfur
and devil, the pinch
of steel between my 10-
year-old fingers. I didn't
seek this, was never good
at hitting body-
sized targets,
kept my eyes
shut while I curled
the trigger. It's heavier
than you think,
to hold and re-
lease thunder.
Not like the movies but
somehow like the movies.
Ears still ringing,
vibrations
in my bones.

Glitch

The night entered me at a bar

in Oakland and I learned that

East Bay is pig Latin for *beast*

and sometimes the hills are coyotes

burning in their sleep and tonight

we need this moon between us

but who knows where this smoke

will lead and try listening to the deep

whistle of a sequoia and know

these Nikes make me feel royal

and curse minimum wage because

forever is tomorrow and today

will fade you without clippers

and patterns will form wherever

you let them because what is

a formula if not this and

who will breathe if you cannot

and where do things go after they are

buried and if bible was really truth

why does our blood hymn and I ask

about the body and I ask as if

you know what I am praising—

Some of Our Boyhoods

Praise the older cousins, the Felipes who intro-
duced us to untouchable things: Lauryn Hill's voodoo

and the deep mouth of Nas;   the rebel
thumb-flicks of a chrome Zippo; scenes in *Full Metal Jacket*

when the soldier explodes his own
face off, before prostitutes

zombie the dark   promising *we love you long time.*
Where we got our cool from, pretended like we knew

what good weed smelled like,   how to slide   a condom on.
Back then, everything   was a series of pretending until we weren't

pretending anymore.   By 8th grade we stopped
doing homework and raising our hands,   instead cutting

class and cracking jokes about the Holocaust
in the back row of history.   No one

to tell us *do your work* or *don't say that*
at home.   We'd just punch and wrestle and shoot

BB guns until birds dropped from the air, heavy   with blood.
The time Jumbo's dog chewed up a kid's hamster and after

the boy cried, Jumbo told him to stop being   *a fuckin' fag.*
How we couldn't watch the hamster's slow unfolding

so found the biggest rock   in the yard.

About *the fierce struggle between civilization and barbarism*

A scientist asked: *Would you sacrifice*
what is known for the unknown?
and I've never felt emptier
though I've searched
everywhere at 3 a.m.
for the stars I couldn't see.
In Athens, my first morning
was a slow-burn of hours
spent wandering the ruins
among other tourists. I learned
something about *centauromachy*
that day: a mythic battle
between humans and centaurs.
It was meant as a metaphor
about *the fierce struggle*
between civilization and barbarism.
That night, the Acropolis glowed
from a window inside
my Airbnb. What I'm saying
is we must all carry
temples holding gods
inside our ribs but we don't
easily open ourselves
for worship. Maybe I'll try offering
myself to your sacred
grounds. Maybe this is a prayer
of cracked palms and you
are everything that is holy
and impossible. Maybe
it's dangerous to look
for the meaning of scriptures
hidden beneath your tongue.
Tomorrow, I'll fly to a nearby island

off the coast of Greece though truthfully
I am always on an island. Truthfully,
there is something about water
I will never trust.
I prefer gardens that grow
whatever sustenance
is needed. Still, I wonder how
our holiness sounds so similar to
our loneliness? I wonder if we'll ever touch
a fourth dimension. I pretend
to be a version of myself
so I can know more
about your world. I am incomplete
and always searching. I sketch notes
in scattered circles
inside a pocket book I rarely open.
How many truths originated
in the most distant places? One day,
let us all return to ourselves. One
day, let us all become the strange
thundering in someone else's sky.

Burning Etcetera

The rain is drift-falling and layers

cannot save me from this winter.

On concrete, teenagers

lean against nothing, Air

Jordans laced and grounded

in a shift of faces. I've asked

if there is an art to dying

this young—if food markets

remind us good times aren't

forever. Yesterday, we arrived

to a chestpunch of dark and cups of red

sangria. We walked

to the farside until we no longer knew

ourselves, until they looked at us

for our tongues.

Pyramids have dusted here

but some still watchdog

the valley, pushing back

against snow.

My days are a murder

of time and watching

the gray slick-slide of trains.

The streets are cigarette-

stained and coffee-mouthed, tired

buildings stiffed against a blue sky.

They remind me of tomorrow's

dark. The people

are friendly and speak slow

when they hear my imperfect

speech. I don't know Spanish

like I know Volkswagens. Like

I know days weathered

as boot bottoms. I wander

the undersides, rub roughness

against my face. Inside

is warmest. I rest my feet

on nothing. What was once

a horse track in Mexico City is now

a public park. Kids and fathers

pop fireworks overhead. It sounds

like warfare. In the morning

we almost got lost

looping dirt paths. I lose myself

in new places. Where you can barely see

it, an old castillo

watches over everything. How

did it end up like this? We came

from Bone Thugs and Selena, a mix

of vibrations in our bonedust.

Rigid is the wrong word

but it follows me

everywhere. I can sketch it

onto buildings, can trace it

around rain clouds. There is a fresh-

ness I haven't known

since last night and outside is a crawl

of wood-

lands growing between us.

Feel what is missing,

make contact without

spitting.

Say *thank you*.

Say *I don't know*.

Say *did you hear that noise?*

These walls are not

really walls. They are

cave mouths, reminding us:

WELCOME!!!

Fuck off media

Beach this way → and I don't know why

I stay inside myself

so often and away

during holidays but I dream

and earlier I blinked

across a border while listening to chatter.

I plucked a book from my bag and let it un-

fold, turning pages

from *Catalog of Unabashed Gratitude*

like a shovel breaking

sun-dried fields.

I palmed the roots,

if only for a split, and stopped

where the outside was a freeze

of glares. For as far as I could

drink there were barely built

things and wargrounds where revolution-

aries once foxholed themselves

the way we must foxhole our desires

at night. I need to know what it means

to be small and sober,

to hold heaviness and hustle it

throughout my bones.

These mountains cannot be overlooked. I cannot

juggle planets, cannot

press rewind and shove it

all back. Where does this weight

on my bone-ribs grow from?

There is no talk of politics

that does not upset me.

I rarely talk loud. I put rocks

in my blood and pretend I am not

fluent in burning tongues.

Self-Portrait as Cartographer

Have you ever retraced the borders on a world
map with your abuela's lipstick? Post-

colonialism is a word that means *re-hustle,*
but should never be re-Tweeted. This isn't

a political statement. The states have been on fire
for as long as they have been stated. What happens

when GPS can no longer locate what you are
looking for? I'm talking cartography,

the fog-swallow of clouds, a wandering
mathematics. Since we've come a long way

from the art of papyrus. Since we've come for more
than your blood can script. Return to your proper

homes. This land is full of forsaken places
I've never visited. What is a sign if it only points you

in one direction? How can you sleep with your eyes
open and an open road ahead of you?

Is it possible to be found when you've fallen
off the map? I've been in wilderness. I've been in fluorescent

cities. I mean this literally—how the lights raged
across both places. How I know the silence

of hands that can draw worlds and hands
that won't even try.

Bricks

Near the park where we hoop
on weekends, we park the car
and spark blunts into rotation like
just-born stars orbiting black
and brown fingertips in a ritual
of smoke-dream and ash. We mix
drinks and debate
Steph Curry, women, Wolverine, never
reaching conclusions. Bored,
we freestyle—I'm in the backseat
of Delande's Buick when a trap
song comes on and my boys
are hype. They rap *fuck bitches*
get money as I peel
my layers off, summoning
spells over trill, spitting rhombus
over rectangle. The cypher
is a loop of infinity and head nods
I never break so bless
the rhythm with intellect
on cue. Halfway through my verse
Kevin turns around and says
Nah, you need to drop
more n-ggas in that. His durag
and gold chain shine in the moon-
light like beautiful armor.
I do not tell him the word is
a brick rubbing my tonsils. That I am
more caterpillar than panther.
I do not say how the syllables carry
more oceans than my mouth can hold.
That I have tried it and drowned.
That I am too afraid to crush the darkness
and the light between us.

Pretty

We'd say *I love you, but not*
in a gay way. High school
kids, we'd only touch

through fist
& gorilla chest
affirmation of man-

hood, avoiding flamboyant
boys like we'd avoid staring
directly at the sun. Now,

grown, I look deeper
as two men inside
Davies Symphony Hall

burn into each other.
How their touch
becomes a soundtrack for their truth.

How they run fingers
in each other's
hair & rub rough neck-

lines like no one else
is alive. Are they unafraid
when saying *I love you*?

It seems orchestral,
boundless, how they merge—
head on shoulder,

hands in laps, lips
slightly apart. *Pretty*,
someone might call it. I say

someone because to say *pretty*
would be *hella gay* of me
& since middle school

I've been taught to never use
umbrellas when it rains, to never
pull from inside your

self for explanation, to never turn
at angles that might expose.
So how do you expect me to say *pretty*?

Leaving Footprints on Waterfalls

There is a voice telling me to hold chocolate

inside my mouth. I don't know what it means.

Like I don't know how lines can break us

apart. I mean this literally. How borders

are thresholds of the imagination. How

some can be crossed. In dreams I wonder

what is real that isn't shared with others.

How we share memories like sweet bread.

How sweet bread crumbles when shared.

How the word *me* lives inside *America* and

in *Mexico*. How I am a forest that grows

after wildfires.

Desert Speech

There is a turtle inside
me crawling
toward you &
this sunlight is Monday
morning slow. Night-
mare scenario
#1: running
out of gas
in the middle.
Nightmare
scenario #2:
running out of
clothes with gas-
oline in my mouth.
Last night too much
drinking. Ironic? Imagine
rain like glitter while Frank
Ocean croons
the boy
of himself
from the chapel
of himself. I am not
a chapel, am more
like the red
rocks scattering un-
interrupted landscapes.
Their silence. Their smell
is burnt
air & nothing
else. The sky's song
always ends
with bruising.
I've listened to it. On road-
trips I've wondered about
the terrain & natives

with skin
like soil. I mean the ribs
& blood of sand.
I mean missing my own
language. These footprints
might lead us where we hope—
because doesn't a pilgrimage begin
once tragedy has settled?
Doesn't dark matter mean
anything else besides *being*
invisible to the entire electromagnetic
spectrum? Space travel
is the geometry of my fingers
against tree bark
holding you up. This is
our version of justice—
how sand dunes
will shift you in ways
you'll never know.

California is turning neon

when Kristian begins to tell me about wild rhinos

wandering Los Angeles. Once, I overheard someone

at a bar say *So much of flying is just getting off the ground*

but after you're up there it's so easy. I don't know

if I agree or if I'm becoming a smaller window of myself.

I don't know what chemicals paint this midnight. I've heard

 a white house screaming at a black one to *get the fuck off*

my block. I've circled wolves inside a strip club while a dancer

told me she wanted a *gang bang in the pussy.* It's nothing

I actually believed. When Ma told me she was sober it wasn't

half-true. Our drunken selves are mumbling

toward a beautiful apocalypse. I can smell the ghosts

of tomorrow like fumes leaking rusted pipes.

What is this architecture? Chances are

we won't meet again if we've never touched

beyond these constructed walls. Hollywood is

a chupacabra we stumble after, after hours. I've seen it

vomiting sidewalks on Spring Street.

Photosynthesis (Chinaka Hodge Hosts a Block Party)

Everything begins by absorbing hydrogen   from dirt as DJs
       spin 90s r&b   with weedsmoke, and wet skin

becomes the oxygen of our bodydance—and it begins
         with inhalation: roots; rhubarb;
         sunflowers; the hot

            stench of chicken mess;
               a thick aerosol

of summer paint; fat

Adidas laces and barbershop fades; the mixing
of light with dark and dark
       with darker. I'll say the names

       of these neighborhood trees out loud:

Southern Magnolia, Maidenhair, Chinese Flame, Kentucky Coffee

       and I'll ask what our cosmology is

if not this—and when I say cosmology know
               I mean blessings,
            and when I say

blessing, I mean this Sunday afternoon, because darkness is a prayer that must come

over us, it is the promise of empty parking lots
filled with movements that can be traced
back to foot-stepped rhythms and chain-link fences, the neon
blaze of a nose ring on a woman's brown nose—

and it begins
         by observing the astronomy of our limbs while

    remembering to sip whatever slow-
honey is poured from your lips

      like the garden in my throat

as your voice
          becomes this shovel   becomes my hands

          digging your waist—

Litany, Ending with Night

The morning air is spiked

with thorns—I am not able to walk

through fire though maybe I have

tried—shame is a parade

of licking tongues and everyone is

invited—ask me if I am

redefining what I know or retracing

false contours—ask me if shadows

are empty or reveal

what is already there—

the translation of being naked

is certainty mixed

with uncertainty—have you ever prayed

in your abuela's tongue?—

there is a sun and a moon

dogging every battlefield—

there is a broken window

inside all of us—the vibes are similar

to "White Ferrari" blaring

from a Chevy—play this on repeat for everyone

to move with—cross the desert

drying on the shores of my lips—crash

your mouth and hipbone

against my dark—our lightning is

a superbloom of waste

flaring into night.

Self-Portrait as American, Pt. II

I am not a god-killer though I've wondered
what I'd wrestle on a Tuesday
in Copenhagen or Marrakesh. Maybe

I know orange fingers and wooden bowls
swirling in a jazz of twilight
while jagged shapes bisect the skies

inside me. There will be no rain-
fall because the clouds will not wash
over my funeral. Give me a definition of love

that isn't castrated. Show me a spade
emblazoned on enemy skull bones.
How can I finish what I have never

been asked to begin? I've declared myself what I am
not: a country embedded
between a splitting torso. Living is a pattern

of sucking air from a room. Sinkholes are nowhere
to be seen until you're in one. These monsters
stalk the fields in my reflection. Do not look away.

Julio César Chávez vs. Oscar De La Hoya, 1996

That night our apartment was an armpit, testosterone
and sweat-washed as if Papi and his friends were the ones

entering the ring. When he let me sip his Heineken I knew
it was a big deal. I stumbled and hiccupped, imitating

Dumbo from the cartoon I'd loved. The men laughed, easily
entertained until Chávez appeared on screen. The *Mexican*

Warrior, they called him. Papi reminded me
how he had battled one hundred fighters, more

than Ali, or Tyson, or Dempsey. Then De La Hoya
entered. Everyone booed, telling him to go back

to his locker like the traitor he was. The Mexicans
thought he was gringo and the gringos thought

he was Mexican. I should've smiled
with missing front teeth for *The Golden Boy*

in his mixed-up outfit, a combo
of US and Mexican flags, but I didn't. I don't

remember the actual fight, a flurry
of blurred punches and card girls in bikinis. I wasn't sure

what took place until everyone on our couch started
grumbling, their movements a slow and beer-confused

disappointment. I swear someone must've cried. Chavez
was hunched over in his corner, right eye swollen

from repeated jabs to the brow, while De La Hoya
stood center, undefeated.

Backyard Boxing

After school we'd slip
    into the back and swing

our skinny: weak
    haymakers we thought

would make us grown
    men. I wondered

if we'd ever get sleepy
    from knocking ourselves

around empty fields,
    if we needed gloves

to shield or break
    us from each other. One

afternoon I refused
    to fight, Emilio's punches

popping my ribs and jaw.
    My arms fell mute

until the crowd lost
    interest. *Hit him back!*

they told me, as if my body
    had forgotten how to hurt.

Shadow Boxing

El cuerpo no es / eterno. / Hoy amanecí con todo / y nadie. / ¿Por qué no hablo direct-

amente? / Mis pensamientos / se pierden como perros / en la calle. Ayer / encontre el

dios de la cuidad y ella no me conoció. / Yo quería dar un beso / a la tierra pero mis

labios ya estaban sucios. / Un pintor me dijo que nunca pintaba / con sus manos. / Autos

viejos nos llevan / a mañana. / Tengo una concha adentro / de mi boca pero no sabe /

cantar del mar. / ¿Cuándo cae la lluvia, qué parte del cuerpo se queda / limpia? El otro

país / me enseño 2+2=5. / Pregúntame / de la alquimia. / Pregúntame si es posible tener

dos de todo. / Las flores caminan solas y mis manos se quedan / sin nada.

Photo for My Unborn Child

I'm riding BART from the air-
port, observing what's outside,
corrugated fences with spray-
painted messages: *This Is Sacred Land;*
Fuck Pigs; Die Techie Scum.
The homes are historic
and diverse as the people who breathe

inside them, colorful and sprawling
along a muscular shore. Your mother
grew up here, on 55th, around the corner
from her cousin's tire shop and the bar
your grandpa would take her to perform
Mariah Carey karaoke as a kid
to crowds of drunken men. The shop

is closed now, and the bar boarded up
with graffiti'd wood. But the house
remains with the ceiling your grandpa
painted as the night sky. We will take you
to see it someday, so you can study
how constellations are formed
from the darkness of our mouths.

Untitled Memory

I'm parallel
parked in a red zone

      on Broadway in front of buildings

with abandoned glass,
waiting for you. No one

bothers or even notices
      my car in the tow-away.

                    It's calm,
            traffickless, nearly perfect

in Oakland. The air is zested

      with weed and piss and other residues
        of someone else's last night.

      From my woofers Frank Ocean's *Blonde*
trebles while between my fingers I flip

    a *West Coast Avengers* comic,
    circa 1984. I don't know why

I occupy this space, a penumbra of what's never been
realer. I don't resist the nearby lake, the clarity of clouds.

               They keep me.

Acknowledgments

To my family and friends. You are all a part of me more than you know.

To all my students over the past nine years, so much love. Special shout out to my Oakland School for the Arts kids, you've all inspired me each day. Isa, the cover art you designed for this book is beyond what I could've ever imagined. Thank you!

Shout out to the readers and editors who've backed me from day one by trusting these poems, often in their ugliest forms. They gave my voice a home and lifted my confidence as an emerging writer. Special thanks to the following journals for publishing earlier drafts of many poems in this collection: *After Happy Hour Review*; *Alien Mouth*; *BOAAT*; *Cosmonauts Avenue*; *decomP magazine*; *Drunk In A Midnight Choir*; *Gargoyle Magazine*; *Ghost Town*; *Hot Metal Bridge*; *Ninth Letter*, *Puckingtown Review*; *Rise Up Review*; *Split Lip Magazine*; *Stars + Lines*; *Winter Tangerine*.

To my classmates and professors who've guided me over the years throughout the Bay Area, New Orleans, Boston and everywhere else I've had the pleasure to learn—D.A. Powell, Brynn Saito, Bruce Snider, Barbara Jane Reyes, Rachel Richardson, Shelby Dale DeWeese, Preeti Vangani, Sage Curtis, Danielle Bero, Todd Follett, Chari Parla, among so many others. You pushed me outside of every boundary I had in place.

To Frank Ocean, since much of this was written while listening to a slowed-down version of *Blonde* on repeat, an audio experience that I wanted to somehow capture. Respect to a true artist of our time.

To Puma, if you're reading this, I want to be the first poet with a sneaker sponsorship, and I'm ready to break into the literary fashion game.

And of course, ultimate credit to my best friend and wife, Briana, for putting up with me and providing endless encouragement and support for over a decade. Since 2008, you've been hitting me with jabs of love and realness, making me a strong-necked kid who can take a punch or two. Maybe even three. (Update: after reading this, she says I can take four). Always yours.

Photo: Briana Chazaro

Alan Chazaro is a former high school teacher at the Oakland School for the Arts, Lawrence Ferlinghetti Fellow at the University of San Francisco, and June Jordan Poetry for the People scholar at UC Berkeley. A Bay Area native, his poems have been featured in the *San Francisco Chronicle*, *Puerto del Sol*, *Huizache*, *Acentos Review*, and *Ninth Letter*.

This Is Not a Frank Ocean Cover Album was the winner of the Spring 2018 Black River Chapbook Competition. Chazaro's debut full-length collection, *Piñata Theory*, was awarded the 2018 Hudson Prize and is forthcoming from Black Lawrence Press. He currently lives in México. You can follow him at alanchazaro.com and @alan_chazaro on Twitter.